*Bardo*

*The Brittingham Prize in Poetry*

The University of Wisconsin Press Poetry Series
Ronald Wallace, General Editor

# BARDO

*Suzanne Paola*

The University of Wisconsin Press

The University of Wisconsin Press
2537 Daniels Street
Madison, Wisconsin 53718

3 Henrietta Street
London WC2E 8LU, England

5   4   3   2   1

Printed in the United States of America

Library of Congress Cataloging-in-Publication-Data
Paola, Suzanne.
    Bardo / Suzanne Paola
    96 pp.           cm.—(The Brittingham prize in poetry)
    ISBN 0-299-16010-6 (cloth: alk. paper).
    ISBN 0-299-16014-9 (pbk: alk.paper)
    I. Title. II. Series
    PS3566.A594B37 1998
    811'.54—dc21   98–23341

*For Bruce*

"And when I love thee not, Chaos is come again"

And thus have you long time undergone suffering, undergone torment, undergone misfortune and filled the graveyards full, verily long enough to be dissatisfied with every form of existence, long enough to turn away and free yourselves from them all.

THE BUDDHA

Suppose Christ should deign to appear here before me, what would he look like? How would he be dressed? Above all, in what manner would he take his place visibly in the realm of matter, and how would he stand out against the objects surrounding him?

TEILHARD DE CHARDIN

# Contents

PART V. *Conspicuous*

# Acknowledgments

Grateful acknowledgment is made to the following journals in which these poems, some in slightly different form, originally appeared:

*American Literary Review:* "Suite for the Child That Refuses To Come"
*New England Review:* "In the Realm of Neither Notions nor Not-Notions" and "Seeing It All as the Bardo"
*Notre Dame Review:* "Tenure at Forty," "Christ in the World of Matter"
*Ontario Review:* "Vishnu Savannah"
*Partisan Review:* "Infertility," "Prayer to Seal Up the Wombdoor"
*Ploughshares:* "Pentecost," "Conception" and parts of "Briseis" (as "Sakti")
*Seneca Review:* "Salmonberries"
*Shenandoah:* "Narcissus: Variations," "Red Girl"
*Southern Humanities Review:* "Deus Absconditus"
*Willow Springs:* "Driftwood Beach"
*Yale Review:* "Fall Landscape, with Empty Places & Sound"

IT TAKES A VILLAGE: A warm thanks to Dan Tobin. And to Robin Hemley, always inspiring in matters of words & greenery.

# Prologue

The bardo in Tibetan means an intermediate state, most specifically the one after death when your soul wanders through the heavens and hells, trying to avoid rebirth into samsara—the realm of the material—and achieve nirvana or Buddhahood. There are lights but unless you resist them you'll be drawn into birth: the green light will draw you into the realm of the animals and an animal birth, blue to the human, and so on. The white light of the gods pulls toward their heavens where you're born as a god, embodied, slowly mortal, still ignorant.

The text, the *Bardo Thöströl* or Book of Liberation Through Hearing in the Intermediate State, was written as a guide. It's read to the corpse for a few days after death (when the soul's in a state of confusion, unaware that it has died), and read by the living. Like everything the bardo journey takes place both inside you and outside. Like everything it's both a metaphor and not.

I was born in the fifties in a nation suspended in the bardo state between a war a decade over and the hellsmoke light of a new war pulling in the East. I became a user of narcotics and high school dropout; later a college student, a journalist, and eventually, a college professor. I can't clearly remember the drug-use time because of the drugs: they seem to have turned life memory into movie memory, with a handful of clear, violent dissociated images and a lot of atmosphere. The time ended with a methadone overdose. Someone slipped me the methadone—which I used a lot anyway—blending it into an orange soda. Slipping it was affectionate not aggressive: my friends and I did it to each other all the time. We called it *dosing* someone, implying that we administered correction, that there was an underlying sickness in the undosed person, terminology the Buddha would have loved—as if we lived unconsciously under the terms of his First Noble Truth, the fundamentality of suffering.

And uncreatedness: none of these people I've been would be able to like or trust one another. The first would spit at the second, the second was always terrified of the last, and the third, like the first, always took what she could get. Along the way I decided I wanted to become a parent and set out my light by the corridor of souls; but I discovered nothing would come. I had maybe used up my allowance for incarnating, for making people out of old flesh.

We learn in the Bardo *life and death happen to us every day, at all times*

Like the bardo of opening a book, of language, which like any light is materiality disguised as something better. The bardo of the lyric, a singular pronoun that leads you in, embodies you, repels you. The self is tangible as well as impossible: I have been someone I'd be afraid of and whom I can't really remember.

I am *is a vain thought;* I am not *is a vain thought*

There are just places entered and left, lives and deaths: the death of turning from an androgynous child to a girl, a child to a Briseis, the faceless female whose loss caused Achilles' sulk in the Iliad. There's the bardo of the eucharist, a liminal place where fane and profane wedge together in the same small molecules. Catholicism and Buddhism cross like electrons in an atom: held by whatever powerful emptiness stabilizes the void.

Desire's the old enemy (*the mind on fire, delighting in the world of multitudinous forms*), something to recognize, writhing in front of us, and overcome—even the desire for nondesiring, for transcendence or the world to be numinous in the theatrical way we think it should be. Because when godhead chose to flow into matter, forcing matter to begin the process of flowing back, it chose the most boring thing present, yeastless bread, a stuff made to stay put, which we eat communally, blank and tasting, as everyone knows, like paper: like the blank pages built into the printing process, front matter and end matter, where the book finally occurs.

*Part I*

# BARDO

So, although this book is ostensibly written for the dead,
it is in fact about life.

FRANCESCA FREMANTLE

# In the Realm of Neither Notions nor Not-Notions


A hawk's rise
over a talus bed by the freeway. Willed
missile of flesh & feather.
Its shadow pumping into the ground
just as furiously—

A mountain road, cut
between talus slopes. Debris
from the cliffs, erosion
flowing
to Lake Coeur D'Alene, *axe-heart*.

A swim of heat
in the air. And a drink
of rock, a river of rock
to drift off on, if
we should abandon ourselves.

❧


Suffering is inherent, said the Buddha,
in all compound things. The trick
to become basic, rendered
like a carcass in a farmwife's hands: into the pot
this huge thing, life, & out of it
a small substance: mostly fat & bone,
fat & bone.

❧


How much heroin did it take to become selfless?
Senseless? A wisp
almost beyond the cold reach of phenomenality?
How much Orange Crush & methadone? I remember
so much just not remembering, a great blank of time
hard & soulless, wonderful

in its purity of conception. Forgetting
how to strike a match, what my hands do.
A place where no Suzanne existed. Years
frozen & gothicked out of time.

Always in language we betray our sense.
*Addict* meaning
the spoken against, the sentenced—

Your bones cry out, your cells
clamor, a bold testament rises in the blood.
This is how the body takes us: *I want I want I.*

How much more can the soul imprison you
with its taste for infinity, its spiritual belly
that expands to the size of god.

Mescaline. A roomful of children staring at colors
scarving from their hands. Heroin. A boy
with a needle just into a vein, so you can almost see
the long ribbon of milky opiate unfolding with pomp
          into the blood—
a swirl, a rapture, like life forming in the womb.

Epiphanies, mystical marriages—

          *Last night we hit a tree*

Sometimes we forgot everything: a boy I was with
lost the concept of *street* & drove his car into a field.
Accidents, fights. Self-
carvers. My boyfriend who slashed a man's hand
off. Frail-veined girls

who shot up in the webs of their fingers,
in the skull behind the ear. Ropes
of bloat on the forearm, friends
who disappeared,

these things were not important—

The one question was oblivion. How to live
anonymous to yourself, a character
narrated by others in day-after phone calls, memory
wholly transplanted to another mind.

> *they said for two hours I threw up, then took my clothes off*
> *& threw up in my sleep*

Did I do those things? Does it matter?
Weren't we unlocked, listening, like an amused
audience at a Victorian salon, to our own adventures?
Slightly bored, slightly formal
with it all.

§

Pale, painted, body
geographic with bone: this girl who lived
as myself—
              She's become
a thing I carry: unsure, watching her sleep
from Coeur d'Alene to Seattle to Bellingham. Hip-
bone, ribcage, imperishable breath.

We looked too hard then: we boarded the wrong ships.
In the one drive
for a stillness so tangible even the shadow stops.

All things, as the Buddha said, of one pure Suchness
*free of arbitrary conceptions derived from sense*

& inconceivable, as a river of rock, as a mountain opening its
              drecked passage,
the small shadow frantic there, & our car's shadow
crossing, seemingly at will, the stygian black.

# Mistaking Opiates for the Clear Light

There's always been this confusion with white things—
hospitals, cold, moonlight.
They seemed to embody the will
paralyzed into peaceful acceptance.
Blank paper consecrate
to the end of words: I love that,
secretly, more than this.
Quaaludes in my palm, rowers, eucharistic form.
Clear bags of heroin.
*Stuff* we called it. Too foundational to define.

❧

In a clear bowl, a pear & a pomegranate wizen
into color. Almost
alive, skins rucking
in on themselves. Cheeks
sunk, russet
& carmine, seeming
almost to care about this . . .
Each a countenance
too private for a face, collapsing
in the hard gravity of color.

I was their opposite, pale girl, not living

or dying. They were
what I feared.

❧

I trust in the bardo wisdom: how the gods,
with their soft white light, draw us in, convince us
their stuporous world is all there is.

I've seen them, slumping
forward, burning themselves with cigarettes.

How grand they were for a while: their leathers, their etched
        bodies, a stalled
writhing eagle on each arm.
And their nectars, their secret foods, that gave
an easy kind of sensate order.

Though a god's world finally
suffers itself away from him, braille of the tracks
of a thousand needles, transgression of red
under the skin—

# Tenure at Forty

November morning in Bellingham, 40
degrees: leafmeal crusted, & frost.
Each step cracks, a little bone.
My neighbors have put plasticene
on the windows for the cold.
I'm checking the thermostat
& the pilot light, getting the flues cleaned.
Thinking of nothing else. Thinking
of how I'm thinking of nothing else—
How the outer life has become
the inner, the skin the body.

I lean forward to adjust the curtain
shocked for once to be *here* & not *there*
to have walked through the six realms
& somehow without knowing it
have chosen
& a corpse lies, done
with her bardo journey

five foot six one hundred
pounds large-boned, each hand
wearing the precise imprint of a lit cigarette
as if glimpsing a future need for proof—

Cliffhanger
without ending, nights
I can't quite remember—
Dragged out of the Capitol Theatre in Passaic by the manager,
        OD'ed, my friends gone.
OD'ed again on methadone, bloody at the lips.
Unconscious in a basement. Awake
in a hospital room. Lyric girl, who leapt

from one image to the next.

Like species consciousness, this memory, like knowing
an earlier stage of evolution—
Neanderthal girl with rabbit fur coat.
The redlipped mammal girl, the reptile

all cold blood & lidless staring.

§

This, then, is narrative.
Ironbluish light
of midmorning. No sun. Nothing that could be called
illumination—
Just a change in tint from the tint of nighttime.
Mountains somewhere
perhaps, their veins against pale horizon.
Neighbors perhaps. Fogbanks
more visible than landscape, more fraught with line.
As if I chose to live where the gods do, veiled
from any overwhelming splendor.

*We're each a piece of spirit*, she said
on television, *we're in, like, a flesh suit.*

I pull on nude pantyhose to stand before the dean.
Tenure meaning *held*. He reads my file

where it ends with Service to the Community (Local)
where it begins, with a name

§

& the letter (we formally recommend be granted)
& my students half
asleep, the room dotted with paper cones of coffee.
Tomorrow & tomorrow & tomorrow. The Psyche
of Keats, Isabella
who planted basil in a pot with a human head, these stories

*The book opens. The cover has bled*
*into the pages. The cover is the book.*
& the story I see in the figure
their bored eyes give back to me—

Middle-aged. A powderblue suit. Pumps. Necklace
of impossible moments.

*I can just see it,* she said.

A woman who came back from death
& couldn't stop telling it, & forgot why.

*Like gloves or something, it just comes off*

# In the Realm of the Hungry Ghosts

When I heard the scrape and singing of last night's dishes
being done, smelled the odor of singed onion
still, when the cat opened her mouth mid-bath as if to
         speak,
& stopped, aphasic, language flooding her
& leaving, I knew that I had fallen through the earth.

Wind drew language
from the trees, from poplars—a leaved
bleat, a melancholy droning.
Dogs sat enviously under the table.

Though no being could argue it had not fed:
shreds of meat soured in dishes
on the floor. Roots spread. Rain fell.
Not a vein of a tree unsatisfied.

I knew then the hungry ghosts
were myself.

Because a pain I couldn't get rid of
kept saying *me, me, me* (the *I*, thin twig
I stumble on) no matter how hard I looked
for the Transparency, kept saying it
in the child I couldn't have, who seemed
in the belly of a pregnant friend to refuse me.

In the books that lay around me: my poems
inked, slick-clad, that became
small mouthings in a dying tongue.
I had everything, & I lay there crying.
I was hungry for things I could not eat.

I wandered in this realm: for a while I played a computer game
where blocky shapes rain down, faster & faster, & you plug holes
 with them.
Always they'd become so fast I couldn't move them, though
my fingers ached with trying, & so emptiness
overwhelmed the screen, & I lost.
Then I started to admire the forms the empty spaces made, shaped
much like the filled blocks, just a little less contained.
More free. Flawed rectangles & squares
 stepping off.
There was little to do then but begin it & watch,

& the solid forms vanished finally, & nothing called to me.

# Seeing It All as the Bardo

In the modern fiefdom of Fred Meyer, the walled city,
where all things necessary exist, & nothing changes—
not in housewares, the supermarket, the pharmacy, the clothing store—
I hear the PA system cry out for Betty Rogers to return
          to Playland,
& I wonder who Betty Rogers is, & why she ever left there.
How human, to wander from a place called Playland

& the voice of the manager
becomes God, & the stiff mannequins of children holding Power Rangers,
seraphim with flaming swords . . .

Maybe Betty is on her knees in the deli section
or found a sacred Ganges in the fountain display.
Or maybe she's dousing her head with charcoal ash from the Weber grill.
Because I too have been rehearsing my sins

in Fred Meyer, on a Saturday.
I can see liver-colored disks of meat
fanned out by the grocery, bins of flame-colored, mammalian romance novels,
a small wetlands of misted seedlings, coppery pipe
ready to take, like the finest confessor, what taints our bodies spew;
a jewelry store, the leviathan-mouth of the door
opening, with its own will, on the half-asleep.

Can it be I didn't see this as a temple?
Can I have missed what my maker so wanted me to see
it just kept repeating
grass-seed, grass-seed, look: litter, look: screw . . .

It's time to publish my sins
frankly, as this newspaper blazons
*Satan's Twins Just Born* to a cow in Minnesota.

When a piece of refuse, gum or candy wrapper,
sticks itself to my shoe, & I kick, over & over again,
to remove it: this is how I've treated my life.

My thoughts have wandered
in every paradise: I've interrupted with my mind
the elegant flow of one thing to the next.
Accused my body of lowering me
when all the time it's been the good servant of an erratic
   master.

And though I've been to the Channeled Scablands & the Eternal City,
driven along Going-to-the-Sun Highway, cruised Point No Point, stuck
my foot in Damnation Creek

I persisted in seeing my life as ordinary,
needing the brush of thought to make it luminous—
the quotes from Augustine, the Meister Eckhardt
consecrating every ordinary act.

I sat in churches, pretending deity can be drawn
from the bulk of its forms, even the windows sealing off
the made world with story,

caging the divine
in those glassy, sad-eyed images
like a too-powerful, too-joyous beast.

§

Along the Diablo lake, we camped
& hiked through the high forest, canopied from rain.
Drew corn & potatoes from the fire
while moths consumed themselves, log-brides
trailing their dirty white garments to the flames—

I knew spirits hung all around. Any minute we might see the dark god,
the one who drinks from a skull of blood. Fanged, fire-
browed, from his home
in the northern corner of the brain . . .

Sagebrush censed the nighttime, Montana dark
spitting out a little matter when our flashlights
            pressed—
dim circle of discolored grass.

We heard the voices of the other shadows
wandering through small pockets of camping space.

*When through intense ignorance I wandered in samsara*

I walked with my flashlight, five
senses & a consciousness. Unable to see. Somewhere

two made love
& I was drawn to them, their stifled shrieks, their *Oh God Jesus Jesus
damn* the way it might have been suffering
but suddenly *I want it*
it wasn't suffering, the labored
excited breath *God it's good baby o* how they rehearsed
*I'm dying here* all the terms of human existence
for the disembodied, waiting at the wombdoor—

Though it seems at the end there's just a silence & a rolling over,
guttering torch, the deep blue human light.

*Now when birth is dawning upon me
I will abandon the laziness for which life has no time
Now that I have attained a human body
there is no time on the path for the mind to wander*

§

Sometimes there's a stammer in my ear
an *I,I,I,I,* bird of self chirping through the lips.
The soft red light of the jealous gods. The ones
who are always softly bickering. A realm

where envy pulls. But I didn't realize
how much & how truly I enter it—

A university. I work here.
My words, the bird says. My
articles. I,I.
High-pitched song
but my own.

*When through envy I wander in samsara*

I come to rooms within rooms, windowless. Thin stick chairs,
like the skeletons of chairs, in rows . . .

And they appear: the goddess-worshipper, the one
whose mother was shot last year, the blind one,
the schizophrenic student with the unpronounceable name
he made up on a mountaintop, & his confession
that he eats ladybugs "because they're beautiful"

*Oh son of noble family, blown by the moving wind of karma*

"It hurts to leave my body," he says, "there's nothing out there
but faces, & I can't look back"

*your mind, without support,*
*helplessly rides the horse of wind*

City on a hill, Fred Meyer, I wondered
where the missing realms lay: I've found them
in your phantasmagoria, your blinking sale lights—
the white light of the gods, yellow light
of the hungry ghosts, hellsmoke light—

And I see the worst thing I've done—
deciding where & when
to pray: carving things up into fane & profane,
as if the self could choose its sacraments.

There's not much time
to gather what I need here. Meat,
butter. A bag
of charcoal stamped with a talking flame.

*When the five luminous lights of wisdom shine,*
*fearlessly may I recognize myself*

& I approach the cashier, hand out, holding a dead bird,
a box of fat, a bag of fire. She takes them
as I give them, her pale, insensible fingernails
dragging them through the sensor to the other side.

I give her money. She lets me pass

*& when the forms of the peaceful and wrathful ones appear,*
*fearless and confident may I recognize the bardo.*

*Part II*

# RED GIRL

There was a great kettle, to set over fire, for the winner.
The Achaians among themselves valued it at the worth of twelve oxen.
But for the losing man he set in their midst a woman
skilled in work of her hands, and they rated her at four oxen.

HOMER

# Briseis

1.

In my small niece's room, the walls
throb pink; pink tights
lie, thrown
on a flowered spread. Rose frills, mauve,
& pearl—
       Girl
colors, blended of blood & milk.
A sprawled doll, & through the window
fat, voluptuous clouds above the sea.

2.

What's better than a woman? said the poster.
Beer—it stays wet
& the container's still worth something after use.

I think about this, in a young girl's bedroom—
how we die at fifteen, the critic said, into symbol

*and turn part legend*
the story of one who waits & languishes,
or flees, like Helen, & destroys.
Of beauty always singular & mimetic—
women roselipped, milkskinned, twinned
& different: Helena & Hermia
*like to a double cherry, seeming parted*

3.

*but yet a union in partition*
so Briseis was led away to take the place of Criseis
Briseis "of the lovely cheeks" lay with Agamemnon
in the hollow left by Criseis "of the lovely cheeks"

maybe the same woman, maybe no woman at all—
except that for Briseis fleet Achilles
went weeping.

4.

To turn woman is to turn
body:
what you are is who's touched you, where they've touched—
*Hey slutmutt. Tease.* Your self bleeds into your fat breasts.
A triangle grows where your legs meet, pointing out
the space you are. Broken,
or intact. A physics of the frangible to learn.

Tampax will break you.
Doctors will break you.
Fingering breaks you.
Menstruating girls kill plants.

*If they're big enough they're old enough we watched girls*
*all day they could of had bags on their heads we*
*wouldn't notice*

off to Agamemnon's camp went the loaded ship.

5.

Agamemnon took her.

& Achilles weeping went
& sat in sorrow apart from his companions
beside the gray sea & the infinite water.

Solitude was necessary
because there was nothing precisely to mourn for—
a chiton that walked, a body
much like many other bodies. Briseis. Easy
dactyl for a blind singer
lost before the wall of a city full of dactyls.

So many lovely cheeks, so many rhyming women.

6.

Mondays at high school
we heard who got their cherries popped
Saturday, whether forced or willing. Some guys said
they'd come in a bitchy girl's mouth, then stay in,
pissing there. First
social studies class: *Rape's
a girl who wishes she said no.*

Question: how & when the rupture.

My friend Alice & I decided we'd do it ourselves, facing
each other, in a dry tub the color of scummed milk—
*scrape around in your cunt with your fingernail* she said *just stick it*
like the Puritan woman who drowned her baby, screaming
now she knew she was damned, crazed with the unlikelihood of election.

7.

Something about the way dolls smile
above their loveable, never-
to-develop bodies—
Pink pink pink pink. I lie here.
This could be my room.

Clouds blown
to a scrawl, over ship-tinged water
like the water where Agamemnon returned the girl, with a message
for Achilles.

That he had not touched her.

Though Achilles knew it didn't matter. She had been sung.
My niece is gone, dressed in a tutu & the black boots I gave her
            for Christmas.
He wept for her, by the pointless shoreline.

# Red Girl

A field. Huckleberry, vetch. The bees' thrum
a tongue of sound licking across it.
Each foxglove flower
choked with a small, trisected body
so the blossoms speak as insects.
A doe looks on. Amazed
at the voice her food has found, its tense, nonsensical
        insistence . . .


§


Under the pier, by glassy rocks, where the Puget Sound
licks its indecision—
arriving with a lunge, crawling out
& arriving—a gray seal
spins. Dead, intact, head caught
where the spume piles, so it's nodding
back & forth, saying *yes*, nodding, for as long as I can
        watch,
back, & forth, *yes*. Exhausting
to see, this relentless agreement,
as if life is No, the capability of No.


§


And the Red Girl. Across
my street, all hesitant, afloat
in my field
of vision. Vivid
mote. Bright cell
in my study window. Cell with its mother's dress
pinned to its nine-year-old body.
An evening gown. Cut to fall
from the shoulders, so she pulls it
up-down, up-down, trying to fathom that. Her lips
smudged an arterial color, & the dress more alive
        even than that living red—

Flame scarf on her hair. Handbag. Evening shoes,
high-heeled sandals, in her arms.
She puts them on & stumbles for a while
as if someone has broken a small bone in each ankle.
Sits & holds
the rust-colored square of the bag
in front of her, a shield
for her lap, a dam there: says *No*
to you, silly seething world, & *No* to you, eye
in the window opposite, that watches me.

Part III

# NATURAL
# THEOLOGY

To the enlightened the world is like a vision and a dream, it is like the birth
and death of a barren woman's child.

THE LANKAVATARA SCRIPTURE

# Conception

From a sparse
handful of seed
comes summer—

Corn and convolvulus. Scatter
of color on the mountainside,
near snow.

*Gone*, we want to say, of some longing
in the slim afternoon—

Though poppies collapse to soft flesh
at a touch, heather
tolls its little bells . . .

A bee, trapped
between windowpanes.
Its three lives
clearly visible—

The past (a meadow)

there, on one side.
The future it wings toward
(bowl of old plums)
opposite,

beyond glass—

Itself at the median point, where *been*
and *will be* strut
and freeze.

So this is the present, this small clear room . . .

§

There were stars, of course,
in some sort of arrangement.
An inch of drink
in the glass. Worn clothes.

A man and a woman lay down together
& three arose.

# Narcissus: Variations

I have set the tray of narcissus
by the breakfast table—
The paperwhites, with their sinning, indolent
      odor.
We follow it, only to find
the massed rectitude of their tall stalks.

Forgive me: I loved their weak mouths,
the one unchanging syllable of scent.
How they punched, greensick as girls,
from their soil. The small

things they told me, the half-truths.

§

You cough in the other room, as you've
been coughing, your whole self
in your throat.

The sickroom smell—night sweats
& sheets, too much
of the human substance—

mingles with narcissus: is drawn
into that almost-artifice, that odor.

§

The rain has begun, Northwest rain
drumming its bored fingers on our roof.
Chronic, as if
something larger than us is bored—

I have set out a green box with white flowers.
What more would it have me do?

§

Forgive me the narcissus:

They seemed to belong here
until I saw the bare maple
through a window—

It splays
against November,
delicate, arterial,
complicated as a flayed body.
Small birds pulsing in the branches.
At the center,
its great, black, ruffling, crow-heart.

§


I have dishonored you with my narcissus—
They stood close to you, frill-lipped:
I set them between us,
a series of arguments against your weakness.

False, you tell me, to fill the eye
with distractions
forced from the bulb, wadded & unmoved . . .

You want courage for me, enough
to fill vases with roses
pendent & withering, stiff,
& set them on tables among our food
so their dying would match our dying.

§

You want me to remove the white flowers.
But I can't imagine
how to live without them: for weeks,
in the blear canopy
of November, the sun

rises as nothing, a flutter in the clouds.

# Driftwood Beach: Theme & Variations


Whiter
even than the starved
matterhorns of the Cascades
gaunted off in the distance: driftwood, forms
of all the creatures nature
never made, casted, cast off: I touch
horn & carapace, even
a pale, fingered sprouting from a bucked branch
that seems, at my touch, to warm.


§


Three lives have escaped
my body, three children
unformed, white, as these—
Unborn, strange to me as this wood,
I touch them here: not in mourning
but a need to take everything back
even pain, so tender when I can see it, horned,
antlered, humped here, like a luminous white fish.


§


I think of the beaches
that made you, children: the beaches
of your ancestors
in Brooklyn, Campania, the sugar
beaches of Barbados, hung with the rum factories'
burnt-sugar smell of cane.
Your great-grandfather, bringing
his touched, Creole
bloodline to America—
The rumrunners, firesetters,
pedophiles who walked before you:
we gather here,
at family, the driftwood beach—

you pull, like the long surf, from our very flesh.

§

*The world is a sacrificial horse,*
I read
in the Upanishads: I rest,
bare-headed, on its bones.
Spittle of sea-froth
at my feet, a heaving,
like pained breath, before me—
Sunset pyres over the western
island.
            Drowned, drowse-
lidded, a young gull rocks in the surf.

What makes this sacrifice, & to whom?

§

Night slips
like a chasuble on a priest's neck,
with votive lights & small incantation—
The thrush has begun again, the Stellar's jay
rasps a syllable of the eighth sacrament.

Be with me, children of the bone—

I name you Grace, & Grace,
& again, Grace; I call you all *Perduta*: lost,
& *Amen*: so be it.

# Infertility

I should have known you wouldn't come here,
where hemlocks point out where the wind goes,
& the sea never stops,
its slap candid as doctor's to infant,
its flood salt & menstrual.

Tell me what keeps you off—
windsound in a gull's throat,
the mad milk of whitecaps, or the trains,
their winching & hauling, their slow,
grunt-wheeled passages.

And the scars on my hands—
How soft & pervious the mother's body!

Child, a strange passion
rules this place.
Breath-holes rising through the surf, through the void
the surf leaves—

while gray gulls
vanish into clouds, as if
some god desired them,

then return,
taut, untouched, still looking.

# Suite for the Child That Refuses to Come

So you've been here before: you know
what you choose against,
I sense from you a *No* both informed & sorrowful.

Out there, where you drift, energy
        without shape, I puzzle you: mother
whose hard labor
gives birth to an uninhabited name.

*Anna.* Part saint, part grandmother, part myself.
It hangs like a sack in front of you, a sack
you won't step into.

Child, I used to torment myself
with the form you wouldn't take: the tiny
fingers, the ten little sequins of nail. Your shape
as spare as my arm.

After that your resistance
taught me to hate my self. My long limbs, the fleshy
spider of my form. Toes, hair, all this pointless
        distinction—
I cleaned
an oily grime off the bathtub thinking *this is my body,*
scurf & surface. *Your* thoughts.
I stopped eating, wanting to be like you. You seemed so sure
of a finer existence.

At last I discovered your fear. How you hovered,
wraithlike, menstrual, above the womb.
Sensing pain there, & a blackish blood
for you to fatten on.

What do I pull you to, from your bardo
of indecision . . .

To delight in bodily form, said the Buddha, is to delight
in suffering

& you wonder at me,
asking you to want this.

I argue with your perfection, the innocence
        you cling to, skyey & unattainable—

Think of god, who could have stopped creation
at a cat, a rose
isolate, without root
or stem, & remained perfect.

Something greater than us
longs for what I offer you: blemish & scar, the wounds
we inflict on what we love, even
the razed ground we live on, the small creatures
that vanish into our mouths.

§

Look around you, child—
the silent one is god.

Not male,
nor female.
Not good.

A thing of emptiness, creating
what fills it.

As if we were to delicately make our own bodies,
whispering the border, the smooth skin,
filling in
lung, womb, the spaces of the heart
flooding & emptying & flooding again.

§

When I saw a young girl living on the streets, ash-
blond, dirty, clinging to her square of sidewalk,
I knew it was you

when I asked her what she needed & she said *Nothing*,
I knew you again,
                        appearing
on the Ave in Seattle with all the other ghosts

to tell me there's nothing I can give you, not even a cigarette
to poison your docetic lungs . . .
Oh, I loved you then, your lips chapped
with the coldness of the upper air, though you wouldn't come.

§


In the ether, in the seventh vestment, in Tushita
Heaven, you wait for me

to change the terms of your residence, to make my blood
spirit, to feather
the hard gristle of umbilicus . . .

For my body, the Hindu
city of nine gates, is a pestilent city—
it should
be walled; everything within

is dying,

but see how it was made
in Eden, with a touch of the finger,
a double strand of acid. A rosary of molecules

to preserve the image, each bead
fragile, liable to be moved—

Even the viruses we get
lie with our DNA, & inscribe themselves.

To be human is to be part god,
part sickness,
always wondering which is which.

*and it was good to see the image*
*lapse, the bone that wouldn't*
*mesh, the blood that wouldn't*
*clot, the omnipotent eye*

*grown vacant—*

And you:
ocean
without shore, unbreaking wave—

Who are you to hold out, in the face of what
without hunger hungered to be changed?

# Prayer to Seal Up the Wombdoor

Because we need to remember
that memory will end, let the womb remain
untouched. Its walls
an image of the earth without us—
No form sharpening, no clutter
of umbilicus,
no fingers diverging from their webs.

Generation is an argument.
It says
my finitude is my infinity: I will shape from it
another & another.

& these will go on, like numbers
that through division can continue, if a little less
each time—

But infants press
against *two* oblivions: the one before,
the one after. And one being
can never outrun two deaths.

Let's celebrate the emptiness, the other place.
Let's create, like God, both void & image.
And carry our end
as we've carried ourselves, in imagination—in film & theater,
statues & mirrors, the long gaze
at our own face.

Look in. See the earth
greening again: closing around
the long bright scars
of cities. When plastic's
rare, an honorable fossil. All glass
finally polished in the sea.

When the reign of the nude skin, the opposable thumb's
over, when the argument runs
whether bones should crouch or stand in the Hall of Humans.

Will it be crows who inherit? With towns
in treetops, winds holy, beauty a pure dull black.
Or beetles, asking themselves
how we ever made love, we, all gravity & heavy limbs.

Maybe by then the fumes of the toilet-tissue plant
will have risen past the atmosphere, & whales will be back,
thick as cattle, with a dim mythology of bloody ships.

Let's insist on contingency, on seeing
our earth is our dream, false
& mutable: blacktopped, split
through the geometries of building & plowing, daylight
dragged into nighttime in small glass bowls.

Let my body stay as it is, saying
we have done our damage, all
in the name of imagination: let something else
through its mind, mar
the surfaces of things.

*Part IV*

# DISEMBODIED

O nobly born, the peaceful deities come from the voidness, recognize them.

From the radiance come the wrathful deities, recognize them.

BARDO THÖSTRÖL

# Salmonberries

It was the redundancy of things
we hated. Not what was in
the world. The way one item pointlessly
became another. The flake of bark that flew
& called itself *moth*.
Unreadable forest, sunlight slipping
down vine maples, rats'-feet bracts
of Douglas fir.

On canes
like raspberry canes, those berries
posing as the soft roe of a suicidal
fish. They crushed
in my hand: drupelets
of that nether-color, not gold, not
blood. Wet
like the inside of the body.
As if to taunt our sense of essence.

I made up a story
of how the fish jumped spawning from the river,
& died like lovers on these thorns.

But they didn't. And no one knows which
is the copy, the above
or below, the one form fattening on its stalk,
or the one in water.

# Columbines

I promised myself I wouldn't love you
anymore, being beyond you: little
spoonfuls of impermanence.
The flowers I could never stop looking at—
tiny flutes honeycombed
with tinier pleating, five
nectar-swollen spurs, five petals
unfolding like a cartoon cry around your mouth.

Such a terrifying articulation of a small idea—

I would never have done
what I've done, if I'd heard you—understood
you, then—what it takes
to make one small, barely visible, quickdying thing.

# Vishnu Savannah

Because this is, after all, a cosmos
essentially trivial, meaning-
less, yet compelling, of a blue
so sentimental any modernist would reject it, our young
& the young of other mammals, ditto, all sweet tuft
& melancholy eye,

we know this is a dreamed world, a great god's,
capable of a great sleep, its thoughts
unhampered by aesthetics, vulgar, rarely ironic.

There's no critic in the realm of creation,
no one to point out
the koala bear is pure pathos, the alligator
melodrama, the Gothic-pointed bat
heavy-handed, too symbolic to be real.

But I wouldn't have suspected
if I hadn't glimpsed things caught
in her eyes—my face, that swart poplar over there—still
in their dark, unfinished state, nictitating,
waiting to be born,

that the dreamer was my cat, Savannah.

Who's herself, in
form, a too-clear reaching after human affections—
Her yowls of needy pride a giveaway, her head
butted into my hand certain
that gods require
a human blessing. That even blessing can be forced.

Of course: only a black-and-white god could be so
color-drunk,
gauding the slash fields with fireweed,
tealing the rim of the sea.

What can we say of a creature
two-thirds asleep, but that she dreams
the real? Waking, now & then, to stalk & play
in the simulacra,
to kill & eat the small creatures of her mind.
Asleep again, eyes twitching, paws
charging in the air, she spins
& pursues &, closing, spins
more years from the infinite for us to run to . . .
Loving the chase, dreaming
the mouse called matter, the mousehole called time, & then _____

# Halfway to the Afterlife

*Proem: Bellingham*

He's across from me, sitting in a chair
when he becomes the chair, or a like substance—
Anyway I see him so: stuff, matter.
A pale fabric racking a brittle frame.
A complexity of parts. A thing that throws
a shadow, just as buildings do. Like
that rubber ficus over there. Man,
thing. A warm mineral crusting with salt.

We made the mistake of thinking we were
consciousness. But I too have felt the body.
Like Daphne's bark it closes over us.
We are stolid as two museum pieces—
antiques, the wreckage of a lost ship.
Someone has propped us into this repose.
I wonder if there's been some error made.
That we are objects without being art.

*Las Vegas*

Sing in me, atoms, who are such a tempting
            emptiness—
(99.999% void space, always shedding, yet
charming when linked in the shape of a man)
of our trip to a place larger than life, or at least
            more brilliant,

& if, in the distance, we see a great pyramid,
Easter Island, if we walk into a room with the David and the
            Trevi Fountain
and a hundred thousand jangling flashing lights
if the presumed dead strut in sequins under their own names,
Frankie Vallee, Dion
& the Belmonts, miraculously here in 1996,
if the real dead can replicate—Elvis on the stairwell,
Elvis in the elevator—
I say we are in
a place transhuman, originatory.

How lucky we are to have arrived here, from the air,
from under a low ruff of clouds.

§

We came from the great blank page of the desert,
burnt red: sands waving up, cresting
& falling, stopped, like an ocean gone to rust.

*Come in under the shadow of this red rock* (the city said)
& I will show you

the same thing, in a new character:
King Tut's tomb, Statue
of Liberty, winged victory of Samothrace—
a Sistine Ceiling on posterboard, all
our bright ideas hiccuped out into the desert.

A Mirage solid in the distance,
full of food & flowers,
a tame volcano, sanctuary where we'll sleep.

§


First comes sacrifice:
sitting on her tripod the Pythia wants
feeding. Images
of the perfect offering everywhere—
dollar dollar dollar dollar quarter dime

At the casino
a woman pours a bucket of quarters
into an oracle's perfectly neutral mouth
as you might fling tokens for a hundred irritable commuters
into a subway turnstile.
It tells her *seven-slash-slash.*

We hold our first day's spendings in our hands—
small rectangles of paper: shreds of material substance.
Something we made & gave value to, as Zeus made humans
& gave us value.

We see that it has made us little gods.

§


Rome, New York, Egypt, the Greece of Pericles
          here—
on the Strip, the realm of forms, the cave's mouth.
We'd seen the shadows flickering & copied them,
embarrassed now, in the face of it, by our efforts.
We got St. Peter's wrong: too huge, too marble, too full of
          mirthless devotion.
The sphinx never had that air of ineffable, half-amused
          sorrow:
he grins like a cartoon cat in front of the Luxor.

The gods themselves walk
through Caesar's Palace & the pyramid, smothered in polyester,
Aphrodite in a sequin-spangled chiton
leading the fat group from New Jersey to a gaming table
& Bacchus with a jug of soda
& the boy Cupid with his quiver of fits.

I am cupbearer. My drink wears a little umbrella
as shield against their brightness.

§

My love is a well-sinewed man, son of drunken
Harold of Glenville, scion of Gay & Zula & Seaborne
Augustus. He clutches his *Winning Casino Play*, a book
black & gold & cunning. A gift from Dawn.
                                          He's woken
from his material sleep. Flips a Bic pen
in coarse circles, so the women in the pit cringe
from the flying instrument as if it were a javelin
flying. He cups

the dice in his hand at the craps table. Blows
on them
          to fill them with the atoms of his breath.
His thinking molecules press into them. He becomes
them. *Four*, he says, *four*, & turns them, showing a two
and a two. The word
made flesh.
Ah, but there is Destiny, mid-air, jumbling his bones.

*Seven Out*, says the stickman, & takes our money.

§

Irrational cruelty—
of course, that's part of it.
A poor mortal weeps at the cashier's booth
of the Stardust. His wig's
askew. The cash machines—
gray, squat, three terrible sisters—
have cut off his name.
Beloved companions: rosy fingered Dawn, the early
rising, always in motion by the great wheel.
Her consort Marc, circling the room
with a glass of foam.

On the barge-stage floating above Caesar's,
Cleopatra waves goodbye to Antony.
Every two hours she does this. They are the forms
of perpetual sorrow. In a slim
wisp of air created to hold
the numinous tragedy of their parting, their lips almost
meet. Then he walks to Nero's 99% Slot Machines
& motions us to join him. We do.
I lose seven dollars. Then win.
Gold showers in my lap, a Danaean rapture.

§

*My purpose is to tell of bodies which have been transformed into shapes of a different kind.*

A line of girls, with trout heads & lobsterheads, dances living before us.
Their legs kick up, slim at the thighs
& at the ankles. Men at the outer chorus, fish-lipped,
golden: my love & I turn
carnal for the monsters before us.

§

Beautiful moments
have been my reason: a crown of sonnets, Domingo
on the stereo, an Oriental fan.
I see that in this, I've dug deeper & deeper
into the mundane world. Not mine to correct
the botched beauties the gods created.

I light cigarettes,
tip a spoonful of whiskey onto the casino carpet.
Libation, sacrificial smoke,

a babel
of beseeching voices, & money, than which
nothing more divine exists, it depends
so helplessly on our belief, & we
on its ability to find us.

§

In the end we're enticed to go upward—
The Stratosphere, A World
Above the Rest: tower
of 300 stories, a roller coaster crown.

Strapped on, strapped in,
winched to the top, plunging & rising again,
we're sequinned, glittering
in a fixed course above the frenzy.
Of human & god & beast.

Noctambulant, constellating, a glide
past Io & Orion, dog star— Set
in the sky, welded
to a beautiful fixed image, our bodies
too fast to move . . . Knowing in this

the gods love us & have finished with us.

*Part V*

# CONSPICUOUS

Gods, though gods, are conspicuous.

HOMER

# Through Glass

*I John saw* (he said)
the heavens resting on a sea of glass
though whether cracked or sure or penetrable
he did not say.

§

My windows deceive me—
handblown, full of the glassblower's flaws:
little faults like seed pearls,
a slow watery distortion
through which things appear, as under a still pond—

I see my garden, my columbines
mouthing their hesitant pastels,
& lambs' ears, the veronica's
blurred blue—

free of the cutworm's trail,
snapped stem after snapped stem,
the spitworm's whittling foam.

My landscape, edited to Eden, from this distance.

§

Closer—
Rose petals cast,
like shreds of flesh, on their thorns.
The funereal in the fullness—
aphids blackening mock orange,
slugslickened trail of gnawed leaves—

& *I* like a stalk, bare of flower & root.

§

This *I* is a myth, a mask.
It's you, if you accept
this instant,
the seedlings placed in your hand
(sage for knowledge, fennel for a lying heart)
which die for you, though you can't see them—
the other can't escape, trapped by these black bars,
but she's not here either, really
(not self, the warm softspreading body)—

no one is here but still a voice returns:
*I saw, I testify.*

§

The sun rises without me
The moon has no thought of me
The crow & the swallow have something else to say

There's always another side to things, & another side,

a glass like the house of language,
a square, like this one, of existence—

Small cap of volcano
under a foam of cloud.
Hummingbirds weaving the air.

Where is the wormwood? The monkshood,
waving its bitter poisons?

Or the rest: odor of lavender,
& sunset, corrosive, brilliant,
over the lashing Sound.

A glass—

Though whether *cracked or sure or penetrable*
I did not say.

꙰

Creator, be afraid of your work.
It has a way of seeing—

Even the crow, from time to time, looks up
with a peculiar wonder

      *(the heavens resting on a sea of glass)*

What voice do you hear, beyond the window?
What watches is watched, always & unknown.

# Pentecost

Cracked Sunday. Babble
of backyard voices
witnessing over barbecue & open flame.

Gulls cry
above the warping, fish-slicked decks of trawlers.
As if they have something to say besides hunger.

I tell you these things, O Theophilus—

so you will know the apostles when they come
swollen-throated on the esplanade's karaoke stand
singing *Volare, volare*

there, where the Georgia-Pacific plant
belches clouds at the clouds,
mimicking the sky, correcting it—

Then motion, an air, a wind—

Why do you stand, gazing up to heaven?

# Deus Absconditus

Late winter, & rain freezes,
thaws, freezes.

Snowmelt
gorges creeks still pushing a glaze of ice—

Withered grass surges in the wind,
& the sky ruts with stormclouds—

*March is the season of return,* I think:
& *Easter,* & *not yet*

What are we, that find words
in this tepid & usual place—
earth, where Edward Hitchcock
saw *emblems of the resurrection*
& Sartre found a dead god in a chestnut tree . . .

These messages
so emptied of content
no one knows how to read them:
whether *weed* grows, or *pearly everlasting,*
whether it's *redbud* or *Judas tree*
that foams to color along the road.

Story without sequence, infinite
story—
    *feverfew & monkshood, resurrection
plant, love-lies-bleeding—*

Earth, my likeness.

❧

At 10, my friend tells me,
Lourdes water healed
her eyes.

Now, sameness & stricture— leafrot
piled in gutterspill, stubble
of clearcut on the mountains. Her eyes wander,
searching for the one sight she was saved for.

Grace, that strikes
like a clock set going—

And the absconded God
who creates
& abandons, leaving us: reflection
of a vanished face,
mirror full of movement in an empty room . . .

I see the first man, first woman
stooped & gray, flaking at the skin—

Perhaps God flew from the image's slow erosion
Or perhaps, like Narcissus, looked down, & drowned here—

# Fall Landscape, with Empty Places & Sound

*Wert thou my enemy, O thou my friend*
*How couldst thou worse, I wonder, than thou dost*
*Defeat, thwart me?*

Wormwood & balm under weeping birch.
A succulent's last, arterial blooms—

Scarf of starlings in the air, undulant, leaving—

Far smoke, pallor & smear
of distances.

Something winged's
sharp, inhuman cry.

§

Poplars shed in the wind.

Like saints dropping a social self, they simplify—

In the same stir
I turn to you,
End of All Myth, One
who makes holes, & fills holes . . .

Were you my enemy
the tree would still turn its jades & shadows in the wind

but nothing would speak
& the salmonrise of the sun would only be morning,

O my friend.

§

You are my sicknesses.
You cut me with the hands of a surgeon.
Miscarrying, I bled you
in thick clots, on a hospital gurney.
You are the dog I brought home, half-dead, eyes kindled, & my
           desire for the dog.

Looking into each thing, I spoke its name.

I have failed in what I tried to do:
I looked for something that is less than God.

&

You are sexless, being-less.
You're not the quick odor of the rose, or its persistent thorns.

Still I call you *master*, because your hand is raised—

Such a healing universe, its thousand things
struggling for a hold, the lame dog
tucking a leg, & learning to run like that—

But full of questions.
unsure, shifting at the edge,

so that the wounds must be made again—
Quick season into dead season.

Gulls yawp, strung
like worn teeth on the power lines.
Crows *awk*, & the porch swing
rasps a vowel in the wind.

Is this the fire, with its cries of suffering?
Or heaven, with its words?

# Epithelial

One thing & then another winnows from the skin.
It's air now, or dust.
Handprints show on the glass vase of veronica.

Sweat from the act of conception
in the rain

We knew this first: the gods toy with us
& change our shape.

& we toy back with them & change their number

Once I sat
on the bitch seat of a Harley, putting
a babysized spoon of powder up my nose.
Once I was a professor in low-heeled shoes.
Demonstrating with a purple chalk how Lear went
          mad.

Winter-skin. Something to remove.
Nothing left. Nothing
but the process & the about-to-die.
The cells that cluster at body's edge, full of
now-useless information—

Faith dries and sheds.
I let it go
only to see it again, turbid &
unsure, doing the old droll
somersaults in a squawk of light.
I scratch my name in the talc it leaves on my writing table.

It will rise, as all useless &
indestructible things do.

We owe God an air to breathe.
The top layer of the soul, the scurf of it.

# Christ in the World of Matter

*The effect of the priestly act extends beyond the consecrated host to the cosmos itself. The entire realm of matter is slowly but irresistably affected by this great consecration.*

With the nightfall that shreds the horizon
with blight twisting the roseleaves
with cutworms & spitworms, summer's
crude instruments of change,
we are one thing, waiting to be turned—

❦

I pull a plant from the ground:
among its roots, a hundred little eyes.

A few tugs on the mass of elliptical leaves
& globes appear, pocked, planetary.
On them, a small woman
pulls potatoes—
Because each thing is both itself & everything.

I am a gardener, I could show you
veronica, valerian, columbine, the foxglove's
stairway of little flutes—

But most of the story, I know, is drought & rot,
leaves tattered by slugs, slugs
hooked & rising,

a jay gawking in my window
at the tomcat, its memento mori,
its end-of-the-road . . .

❦

Because I saw a crow in the wind
that dragged itself from a giant fir—
rising in a squall,
it flapped wildly, never moving, then,
exhausted, dropped back,
rose again, stalled,
& again, stalled,
as if doing it for me, though of course
*me* is absent there, in that leaved, tree-level,
too blue crow-universe—

*Because I saw a crow in the wind*

I knew that was the soul, that restless thing,
the thing that is said *no* to—

& it repelled me
with its longing, the stupidity of its longing.

§

Call it
the *undersoul:* the life in each grain of matter.
Not just the bird but its brains,
lungs, barb & vole
of its feathers, each
molecule that pushes into the wind—

The hopeless, whirling, Paolo-and-Francesca embrace
of proton & electron.

Endless fighting, endless flux—

Things that cannot stop, even in our mouths,
becoming other things—
*Valerian, valediction.*
*Sorrel, sorrel, sorrow.*

§

The unsayable brevity
of *now*—

Can you feel it?
Can I even tell it fast enough?

The three seconds of the present
gone before you can touch them, almost before
you can listen . . .

So the seagull's pure *akk*
disappears into story—

(a cry like the cry of a baby,
a screech like the screeching of wheels)

The past a story
we tell ourselves, the present
a story we are told—
Consonants of cabbage worm, vowel of blood . . .

Black earth
where something lives
that feels so able to speak

we say *mouth, mouth*
of every rupture in its surface—

*Mouth* of volcano
though the boiling, laval tongues
consume their own silent throats.

Mouth of a cave
in which a tomb is found empty.

Appearing, leaving:

I only know a banquet's been given,
a Roman banquet, full of dancing & grief,
& the giver at the last minute hurried upstairs,
declining to sit at table . . .
Then temptation drifted up
(an odor, a low sound)
& someone came finally—

We called him incarnate, *Made-Meat*.

Like a man, he carried his sex
in the open. Like a woman,
he would bleed & return.

We said, we have one gift, something
you must envy, we call it *death* . . .

It will fill your days.

§

The monk said, all matter was transformed
in that instant, in the virgin's womb,
when infinity congealed

to a clot of blood.

Like thought flowing into language,
the elasticity of the abstract
gone, pushing itself

into shape.

But the bloodclot, too, was changed, each molecule
feeling that other possibility, divine,
uncommitted existence.

Face
without bone, sex

without gender, a god
like a cup's expectancy,

perfect emptiness.

What we call human
begins here . . .

Where god turned boy, baptized
into appetite,
& rose, keeping

the stark souvenir of his body,

Misericordia,
Moment of grief to slip back into
somewhere at the end of time . . .

*Notes*

# Notes

PAGE 3. "The Realm of Neither Notions nor Not-Notions": the highest of the heavens, beyond physicality, and deceptive because it can be mistaken for nirvana.

PAGE 11. "The Realm of the Hungry Ghosts": one of the realms of the bardo. The hungry ghosts have enormous bellies but almost no neck, so are unable to eat.

PAGE 13. "Seeing It All as the Bardo": interpolated text is from the *Bardo Thöströl* (commonly translated as *The Great Liberation Through Hearing in the Bardo*), Fremantle/Trungpa translation.

PAGE 21. "Briseis": Agamemnon, forced to relinquish his trophy Criseis to her priest-father, takes Briseis from Achilles in compensation and starts the feud that constitutes the *Iliad*. "The critic" is Denis Diderot. Helena and Hermia: characters in Shakespeare's *A Midsummer Night's Dream*.

PAGE 51. "Vishnu Savannah": Vishnu, the Hindu preserver god, dreams the world and keeps it in motion through dreaming.

PAGE 53. "Halfway to the Afterlife": "My purpose . . .": Ovid's *Metamorphoses*. The Pythia: the great seer at Delphi.
    This poem is dedicated to Bruce, craps shooter extraordinaire, and to Dawn Dietrich and Marc Geisler, who really understand Las Vegas.

PAGE 61. "Through Glass": The first two lines are adapted from the Book of Revelation.

PAGE 67. "Fall Landscape . . .": The quotation is from Gerard Manley Hopkins.

PAGE 64. "Pentecost": On Pentecost the Holy Spirit descended on the apostles, causing them to speak in the tongues of those around them. Theophilus, whom the author of Luke/Acts addresses, means God-Lover.

PAGE 71. "Christ in the World of Matter": The quotation is from Teilhard de Chardin's *Hymn of the Universe*, as is the quote of Teilhard's at the beginning of the book.

## The Brittingham Prize in Poetry

The University of Wisconsin Press Poetry Series
Ronald Wallace, General Editor

---

*Places/Everyone* • Jim Daniels
C. K. Williams, Judge, 1985

*Talking to Strangers* • Patricia Dobler
Maxine Kumin, Judge, 1986

*Saving the Young Men of Vienna* • David Kirby
Mona Van Duyn, Judge, 1987

*Pocket Sundial* • Lisa Zeidner
Charles Wright, Judge, 1988

*Slow Joy* • Stefanie Marlis
Gerald Stern, Judge, 1989

*Level Green* • Judith Vollmer
Mary Oliver, Judge, 1990

*Salt* • Renée Ashley
Donald Finkel, Judge, 1991

*Sweet Ruin* • Tony Hoagland
Donald Justice, Judge, 1992

*The Red Virgin: A Poem of Simone Weil* • Stephanie Strickland
Lisel Mueller, Judge, 1993

*The Unbeliever* • Lisa Lewis
Henry Taylor, Judge, 1994

*Old & New Testaments* • Lynn Powell
Carolyn Kizer, Judge, 1995

*Brief Landing on the Earth's Surface* • Juanita Brunk
Philip Levine, Judge, 1996